FOREWARD

This story was inspired by real life events and personal experiences with relapse.

Before reading, please be aware that substance abuse affects everyone differently.

There is not just "one path" to addiction or relapse and there is not just "one cure"; different treatments work for different people.

Sobriety is also different for everyone. Some people are still able to drink or smoke etc. while abstaining from their drug of choice.

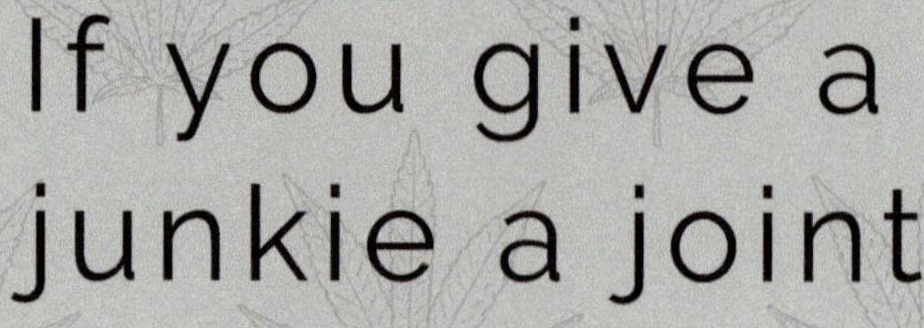

and he decides to
smoke it...

If he drinks beer....

...He will want
liquor.

...If he drinks
liquor...

...he will want to snort cocaine.

That's some good $h!!!.

If he snorts cocaine...

he will want to
smoke crack.

After he smokes
crack...

he will need to
snort heroin...

...until his nostrils
blow out...

Then he might
switch to pure
fentanyl....

...or he might start injecting meth, because it's cheap.

...Then he might alternate between meth and heroin...

until he runs out of
money...

...but he needs
money to buy
heroin...

so he sells his
possessions.

Once he has sold everything he starts to steal...

he steals from you, from friends, from family, from kids, from strangers, from businesses...

he does whatever it takes to get more drugs.

He loses his house, his job, his family, his friends...

what happens next?

what happens
next?

He dies from an
overdose...

he goes to jail or prison...

he is
institutionalized...

he is killed during a
drug deal gone
wrong...

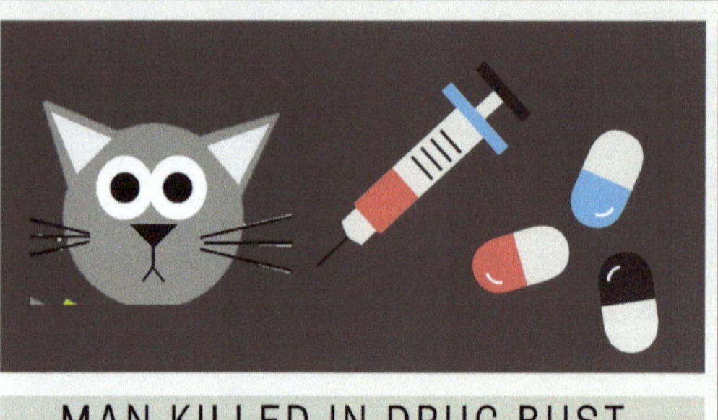

OBITUARY
MAN KILLED IN DRUG BUST

he is robbed and killed
for drugs or money...

he is killed during a psychotic episode...

i have to kill all the aliens! they are coming
SIR - DROP THE KNIFE AND GET ON YOUR KNEES

he commits suicide...

or...

he accepts help and
decides to get sober!

THE

END.

TO ALL THE RECOVERING ADDICTS,

DON'T FORGET TO PLAY THE WHOLE TAPE WHEN CRAVING STRIKES.

Although this story's main character is a "He," substance abuse can affect anyone. This disease does not discriminate based on sex or gender, race, ethnicity, occupation, age, socioeconomic status, or geographic location.

IT'S NEVER TOO LATE TO GET HELP

IF YOU OR A LOVED ONE IS CURRENTLY STRUGGLING WITH SUBSTANCE ABUSE, THERE **IS** HELP AVAILABLE.

FOR TREATMENT REFERRAL PLEASE CALL:

SAMHSA'S NATIONAL HELPLINE (U.S. ONLY):
1-800-662-HELP (4357)

VETERANS CRISIS LINE (U.S. ONLY):
1-800-273-8255 (PRESS 1)